PREF

THE following chapters are a reprint of papers published in *Commonwealth*, mostly in 1896. They are reprinted at the request, and under the management, of one of the Editors of that magazine. The text of the Lord's Prayer employed in them is that of the Revised Version.

I should like to call the attention of those who desire practical assistance in praying on the model of the Lord's Prayer, to the blank outlines for prayer, personal and intercessory, in the late Mr. Bellars' *Before the Throne.*

C. G.

Lent, 1898.

CONTENTS

1 MONTH OF
FREE
READING

at

www.ForgottenBooks.com

By purchasing this book you are eligible for one month membership to ForgottenBooks.com, giving you unlimited access to our entire collection of over 1,000,000 titles via our web site and mobile apps.

To claim your free month visit:

www.forgottenbooks.com/free70306

ISBN 978-0-483-61499-4
PIBN 10070306

Forgotten Books is a registered trademark of FB &c Ltd.
Copyright © 2018 FB &c Ltd.
FB &c Ltd, Dalton House, 60 Windsor Avenue, London, SW19 2RR.
Company number 08720141. Registered in England and Wales.

For support please visit www.forgottenbooks.com

Prayer

and

The Lord's Prayer

By

Charles Gore, M.A., D.D.

Of the Community of the Resurrection
Canon of Westminster

London

Wells Gardner, Darton & Co.

Paternoster Buildings

1898

Prayer, and The Lord's Prayer

I

The Efficacy of Prayer

IF a man regards the thought of Christ and His apostles as in any way representing spiritual truth, he cannot but own that among the most powerful and rich of human faculties is the faculty of prayer. It is not necessary to quote passages from the New Testament to prove this. But certainly if it be true that the faculty of prayer to God is thus powerful and rich, it is also sadly true that, in our modern world, the pains bestowed upon it are not at all proportionate to its value. Nor can it be said to be properly appreciated in our ordinary estimate of things. We think of the men and women of scientific intellect, of eloquence, of artistic genius, of political and social activity, as being our powerful men and women, rather than the diligent and constant offerers of prayer. Truly from this point of view 'the world knows nothing of its greatest men.'

And our Lord at least hints to us that so it would turn out. He describes under a startling figure the effectiveness of importunate prayer, and at the same time forecasts the strains it will involve on human faith. The effect of importunate prayer upon God is compared to the effect of the widow's importunity upon the unjust judge. The conclusion is drawn. 'Shall not God avenge his own elect, which cry to him day and night, and he is long-suffering over them? I say unto you, that he will avenge them speedily. Howbeit, when the Son of Man cometh, shall he find faith on the earth?'[1]

I repeat the question and apply it. Does He find faith, the faith which shows itself in systematic prayer for the coming of His kingdom, now in our time, on our earth? If He does not, who can express the peril and the loss? Who can deny that we are ignoring one of the three constant elements in normal human life?

We look at human life broadly, in the long reaches of history, and you observe it moving in three different directions. It moves out toward nature to appropriate its resources, and the history of this movement is the history of civilization. It begins where the savage feeds on berries, or hunts his prey, or scratches the surface of the soil to throw in his seed; and it advances to the point of almost inconceivable power, skill, elaborateness,

---

[1] St. Luke xviii. 1-8.

2

and subtle balancing of forces, which characterizes our modern industrial system.

Secondly, we watch man moving out to develop his relations to his fellow-men. It is the history of society, beginning with the tribe and the family, and reaching up to the social organization of to-day, with its breadth of range and intricacy of relationship.

Thirdly, we watch mankind moving out towards God. The movement, looked at in the broad, is quite as perceptible and as important as the other two movements. It occupies, like the others, a large share of human effort and attention. It passes through similar stages. It has its rude beginnings in savage religions, as men 'ignorantly worship' or 'seek after God, if haply they may feel after him, and find him.' Like civilization and society, it has taken many different developments. But the aim of all these different developments of religion, and of prayer, which is the most characteristic act of religion, is realized in the religion and the prayers of the Son of Man, and of that great catholic brotherhood which in His name worships the Father in Spirit and in truth.

We are the 'heirs of the ages' in the matter of prayer, no less than in the matters of civilization and society. But the question is, whether our zeal is in proportion to our knowledge.

I remember once, in the early summer of 1884, seeing a sight in India which made a permanent impression on my mind. In the modern busy street in Calcutta, called Bow Bazaar, in which the Oxford Mission House used to stand, I saw by the side of the tram-line a man, stark naked, with chains round feet and hands. He was lying flat in the dust, measuring his length on the ground. He rose as I was looking, advanced a few paces, and standing upright, with his feet where his nose had marked the dust, he prostrated himself again, and proceeded to go through the same motions. He was a fakir or devotee of some sort, and I was assured that he was going to travel in this manner all the hundreds of weary miles which intervene between Calcutta and the sacred city of Benares. My first feeling was, I fear, one of disgust and contempt at the superstitious folly of the man. But I hope it was soon overtaken and checked by a consideration both worthier and with more of humility in it—the consideration, I mean, that he, in his belated ignorance of the character of God and of the way to serve Him, was taking a great deal more pains about his devotions than I was in the habit of doing with my better knowledge. This is the question for us: Do we, with our superior knowledge of God, take trouble about our devotion to Him, or put real effort of will and heart and head into it, at all proportionate to the true knowledge granted to us, at all proportionate to the amount of effort we put into our businesses or our social duties and pleasures? Or is our life of business and our life of pleasure organized and real, and our life of prayer

4

limited to a rather perfunctory hour on Sundays and a few of the sleepiest moments of our day ?

Undoubtedly, if we have the privilege of intercourse with God, we must take pains to realize it. Undoubtedly, if there is a life of prayer, it will not be experienced or developed without real effort and system and thought and perseverance.

But to justify us in taking pains about prayer, we must believe in its efficacy. I cannot seriously train myself to hold intercourse with God, or make request to Him, unless I really believe both that God exists and that He hears and grants the prayers of men. Now comparatively very few people doubt the existence of God, but a great many people doubt whether He really hears and answers human prayer, and accordingly, whether it is worth while taking pains about prayer.

The difficulties most commonly experienced are perhaps these—

1. It seems inconceivable to our 'common sense' that God, the ruler of the vast universe, should have a personal relation to each individual, such as the belief in prayer requires—a personal relation implying a particular care and a particular providence. Like the man whom the son of Sirach reproves, we mutter, 'Who shall remember me from on high ? I shall not be known among so many people ; for what is my soul in a boundless creation ?'[1] And no doubt to *conceive* how

[1] Ecclus. xvi. 17 (R. V.).

the mind of God can attend to every one of the innumerable individuals who make up the universe of men (to say nothing of other existences) is impossible to us : that is, it is impossible to imagine it or form a picture of it in our mind. But our imagination is very far indeed from being the limit of our reason. There are many facts forced upon us by the science of astronomy, or physics, or chemistry, which we cannot *imagine*, but which we are rationally compelled to *believe*. So it is with regard to this difficulty. Our reason demands it, though our imagination is baffled. For let us think. To get to know anything better is to get to know it more widely, but also more in detail. The school-master not only knows boys, but knows his own class of boys better than another because he knows them individually. The great generals are distinguished like Napoleon for nothing more than this—their combination of widest conceptions and plans with attention to the smallest details. To know well, therefore, is to know both broadly and in detail. And to act well is to act with a wide grasp, and also an insight into each individual case. So we must grant that the absolute perfection of the knowledge and action of God must mean that the universal range or scope of the divine attributes, over all creatures whatsoever, diminishes nothing from their perfectly individual application. God—our reason assures us, though our imagination is baffled—must know each of us and love each of us as if there were no other in the world to know and love, and deals with each of us with an individual providence, in which His universal laws or methods of action are not violated but expressed and exemplified. That is the verdict of reason, and it is also the assurance of Christ. 'The very hairs of your head are all numbered.'

2. 'But, granted that God knows all we want, and wills to give us what is best for us, what is the use of praying?' To ask this question shows indeed a fundamental mistake as to the purpose of prayer. No doubt it is the judgment of reason, as it is again the assurance of our Lord, that our 'Father knoweth the things we have need of before we ask him,' and knows them a great deal better than we do. The object of prayer is not to inform God or to correct His methods—to drag down His wisdom to the level of our folly : the object of prayer is to educate us in intercourse with God. We are sons of God, capable of something better than mechanical obedience; capable of intelligent correspondence with our Father, capable of fellowship and communion with Him in one Spirit. There is to be what the New Testament calls 'freedom of speech,'[1] and an open avenue of 'inquiry towards God.'[2] That is our highest function; and that is the glory of our eternal occupation. To train us for it now, in the child-

---

[1] The word translated 'boldness' in Eph. iii. 12 ; Heb. iv. 16; 1 John iii. 21, etc.

[2] 1 Pet. iii. 21 (R. V. *margin*).

hood of our immortal life, even though we babble with half-inarticulate sounds, we are to be practised to pray. We are to ask persistently and regularly, and according to the loving wisdom of God, to receive in response to our prayers, and so to be educated into personal relations with God.

Who can deny that the end is worthy? and who that has ever taken pains about prayer, or 'got an answer,' can deny that the method is wisely chosen?

3. 'Ah! this kind of argument was all very well before it was known that the world was governed by fixed laws; but now that the universal reign of law is recognized, we cannot believe that our prayer can have power to alter it, or affect the course of nature as it moves on in its inexorable order.'

This is an objection which it is better to press a little further; and, as in many like cases, if we press it to its consequences we may be enabled to see that it will not hold. So far as it implies that we cannot hope to alter the universal laws of nature, it is certainly valid. Any prayer which is an attempt to alter the laws of God's natural government, or to drag down His wisdom to the level of our short-sightedness, must undoubtedly fail of its purpose. We do know that the world is governed by fixed laws, that is, that God's method in governing the world is a method of universal law or order. But because the world is governed by fixed laws, does it follow that nothing is left to our action? That the

8

laws work on without any possibility of fruitful effort or co-operation on our part? It is in accordance with fixed laws that gold is extracted from the earth and turned into coin. But will this happen unless we discover it and extract it, and put it through all the processes of manufacture? Needless to say it will not. Here we touch the mystery of free will: namely, the fact that within certain limits the way the world shall go depends on our action or inaction. I make here no kind of attempt to solve this mystery. I only insist that the responsibility involved in our freedom is a practical truth—that though the world is governed by fixed laws, a vast deal of the utmost importance to us depends on our co-operation and correspondence with the system of nature.

As the great Francis Bacon taught the world, the secret of power in nature is correspondence with its laws. It was exactly the same lesson which Jesus Christ taught the world in relation to prayer. Prayer is fruitful, and is offered in 'spirit and in truth,' exactly in proportion as it is not an attempt to fight against the laws of God's good government, but an attempt to correspond or co-operate with His purpose. Christian prayer is one way of correspondence with God. And there is—I say it with perfect confidence—no greater difficulty in believing that God intends to give us whole classes of good things for soul and body, but will not give us them unless we correspond with His purpose by diligent prayer, than in believing that whole classes of good things are stored up for us in nature, which will not be our own unless we seek them by diligent hard work. There is no more difficulty to our intellects in one kind of co-operation than in the other.

We accept the fact that if we want wealth we must work for it, though we cannot explain how inexorable laws leave room for human freedom. We can, with exactly the same reasonableness, accept the fact as practically true, that there are multitudes of things which God means to give us, but will not give us unless we pray for them. This fact of the efficacy of prayer rests on common human experience, on the witness of experts, that is, of especially spiritual men and women, and, most of all, on the authority of the Son of Man.

But here we touch the question of the grounds for praying, and of the difference between ignorant and enlightened praying—the praying which is 'in the name of Christ'; and we must leave the matter for another paper.

II

Prayer in Christ's Name

I

IN my last paper I pointed out that prayer, in its
various forms, appears to be as truly a natural function
of human nature as the promotion of civilization or
of society; and this itself is a powerful argument for
the reality of the Object of prayer. We find the men
of science constantly reasoning in this manner. If
they see any organ or function in any plant or animal
strongly and constantly developed, they infer that there
must be something in nature, external to the plant or
animal, which renders this organ useful; for nothing,
they assure us, can become developed and maintain
itself, unless it is in real correspondence with some fact
or facts of the external world. To take only one
example, the eye is an organ which has developed and
become a constant part of animal organisms. It could
not have done this unless there was a reality called
light external to the animal, such as justified the

existence of the eye, and made it useful. We may argue in exactly the same way. It would have been impossible for man to appear constantly and persistently in the attitude of prayer, and for this religious tendency to take shape and become persistent, unless God, the object of prayer, were a reality, and man by praying was brought into real and profitable relation with Him.

And the force of this argument is increased when we observe how the prayers of mankind pass through many stages, in which they seem to be 'feeling after' their object without truly 'finding' Him, till at last, through the teaching of the Son of Man, they appear to attain for the first time to real correspondence with Him. This, I say, increases the force of the argument, because it is what we observe in the similar case of the investigation of nature; and in this respect we may compare, as has been already suggested, the place of Jesus Christ in the history of prayer with the place of Francis Bacon in the history of science. There was investigation of nature before Bacon, for nature is inevitably fascinating and alluring to the imagination of man, but through fifteen centuries it had made no progress. Why? Because it made no serious attempt to be in correspondence with the reality. It was seeking to impose men's arbitrary whims—the whims of the astrologer and the alchemist—upon nature. It was seeking short-cuts to universal knowledge—the philosopher's stone, the elixir of life. It was arbitrary, therefore it was unprogressive. Now Bacon made no progress himself in the knowledge of nature; but as a sort of prophet he put into words the principles which ought to guide men in their inquiries. 'Nature,' he said, 'can only be controlled by being obeyed.' 'He that will make progress must enter the kingdom of nature a little child.' The reverent investigation of nature as she is, and the power won by submissive correspondence to her actual laws, these were to be the watchwords of scientific progress. These, in fact, have been the watchwords of that gigantic advance, both in the knowledge and use of nature, which has characterized the last three centuries. The reverent investigation of what nature's laws in fact are, has resulted in the forces of steam and electricity being at the disposal of mankind.

Now, as in many other respects, so also in this—our Lord differed from Bacon in that what He taught He practised, and what He professed He realized. Still, we may find in Bacon's teaching in regard to the knowledge of nature, a suggestive analogy to our Lord's teaching in regard to the exercise of prayer. Prayer, before Christ, had expressed the indomitable human instinct which drove men to seek relations with God. But it was ignorant asking. Christ, by His teaching and by His atonement, first put the instinct into perfect relation with its object; into perfect relation both of

13

knowledge and of power. He taught men the character of God the Father. He taught them about human nature, its capacity and destiny, the meaning of sin and the remedies for it, the true use of physical pain, the fruitfulness of sacrifice. He assured men of the final victory of the divine kingdom, and pointed to the Church as the society which is to represent that kingdom in this world, and to prepare the way for the kingdom which is to come. By all this body of teaching He did not, indeed, satisfy human curiosity about divine things, for He still left man largely under the discipline of ignorance. Still, 'we know in part,' we 'see through a glass darkly.' But He did put us into a correspondence, which is adequate for practical purposes, with the mind and character of God. Henceforth prayer can rise in real correspondence with known truth, in the face of enemies whose nature and the limitation of whose powers have been disclosed to us. It can rise in accordance with the laws of the revealed kingdom of God. In a word, prayer has become intelligent correspondence with the manifested God, the correspondence of sons with a Father.

II

When you examine the utterances of Christ with regard to prayer, you find that they consist of large general promises, subsequently defined and made more exact. 'Ask, and ye shall receive.' Here is a large general promise. It arrests the attention by its obvious contradiction to facts of experience. It stimulates further inquiry, and further inquiry is met by exacter statements. 'Therefore I say unto you, all things whatsoever ye pray and ask for, *believe that ye have received them, and ye shall have them*' (St. Mark xi. 24). Again, '*If ye abide in me, and my words abide in you,* ask whatsoever ye will, and it shall be done unto you' (St. John xv. 7). Once more, 'Verily, verily, I say unto you, if ye shall ask anything of the Father, he will give it you *in my name*. Hitherto have ye asked nothing *in my name*. Ask, and ye shall receive, that your joy may be fulfilled' (St. John xvi. 23, 24). When we come to consider them, these further definitions of the conditions of prayer are found to be in close agreement. Thus it is morally impossible to have a real confidence that the things we are asking for shall be certainly received, unless our petitions are grounded on some real knowledge of the mind and method of God; otherwise asking would be a mere crying for the moon. Thus the first of these passages

15

is in correspondence with the second. The prayer which secures its own answer is the prayer which is determined by the mind of Christ, the prayer which expresses not our own lawless and short-sighted wants, but the will and purposes of Christ, who is the image of God; the will and purposes of Him whose victory was the victory of complete self-surrender, and whose triumph was the fruit of what in the eyes of men was completest failure. And this is what our Lord means by prayer in His name. It is a childish fancy that we pray in Christ's name by adding the words 'through Jesus Christ our Lord' at the end of any petition we like to offer. The name of God, the name of Christ, in the New Testament expresses something much more than certain syllables uttered by the voice. They express the being of God as He has revealed Himself in Christ. The ambassador who speaks in the name of his country or his king, does so because he represents not his own views, but the views of the power which sent him. Thus, to pray in the name of Christ, is to pray as one who represents Christ, whose mind is Christ's mind, his point of view Christ's point of view, his wishes Christ's wishes. With what force will now come home to us those words of Christ, 'Hitherto, have ye asked nothing in my name.' So many things we have asked, but in our own name. Perhaps we have not prayed for many years with any reality, and then some calamity seems ready to fall on us. We

16

fling ourselves on our knees, and pray, 'Oh, my Father, avert from me this blow which I so sorely dread,' or 'Give me this boon which I so greatly desire.' There is value in all serious approach to God; but this sort of prayer, which is selfish, and is strictly from our own point of view, is not prayer in Christ's name, though it may end up with the accustomed formula, 'through Jesus Christ our Lord.' Nor, if our friend or child is sick unto death, and we pray with tears for the sparing of his life, is such prayer prayer in Christ's name, unless we have really risen to take His view of sickness and suffering and death. Now we see that prayer in the name of Christ is something which can only arise out of a will and heart redeemed by Christ, and brought by Him into union with God. It is the prayer of moral correspondence; it is the prayer of sons.

III

But here a number of questions arise. We may fairly ask, what are the subjects of prayer in Christ's name?—what can we pray for, and what can we not, in accordance with His will? For instance, may we pray for health, for fine weather, for physical as well as spiritual blessings? To these questions in detail I propose to attempt an answer in the next paper; but meanwhile I will point out, that our Lord did not leave this matter in the region of abstract speculation. He taught us by example. 'After this manner, therefore, pray ye.' The Lord's Prayer is not so much one prayer among many, as the type and pattern of all Christian praying, and if we want to know whether any prayer can be truly described as a prayer in Christ's name, we had better ask ourselves whether it can fall within the scope, and be expressed in the language, of the Lord's Prayer. Indeed, the lessons of prayer find in the words of that great example their deepest expression. There is both the full realization of the broad human instinct of approach to God, while at the same time there is the sternest rebuke of the selfishness and the narrowness which ordinarily mix with it. The prayer of untaught human nature is, 'My Father, give me to-day what I so sorely want, avert from me what I so utterly shrink from.' The very order of the Lord's Prayer, apart from the meaning in detail of its particular clauses, strikes the broader, the diviner note. 'Our Father,'—the very first words are the rebuke of selfishness. They force us to place ourselves before the impartial God with whom is no respect of persons, whose thoughts are higher and purer and wider than our thoughts, as the heaven is higher and purer and wider than the earth; but who yet is near to us with all the individualizing love and care which belongs to His fatherhood. ' Hallowed be thy name;' that is, let God's revelation of Himself, His truth, His character, be held in honour. That is the first petition. Probably there is no man, however spiritual, who in the present age would have put this petition first. The honour of God's truth is so continually, in the modern mind, subordinate to human needs. But in the Lord's Prayer we are first forced to exalt into the place of supreme importance the unchangeable honour of God Himself. 'Thy kingdom come.' We are interested in our narrow schemes and wants, but here we are forced to merge our littleness in that great and divine purpose, which through all the ages is slowly realizing itself. No self-centred will or desire can hold its own here. 'Thy will be done.' We are forced to bend our stubborn wills and inclinations until they are brought into conformity to that great will of God, to which all the hierarchies of heaven find it their joy and glory to minister. Only then, when we have exalted God's glory above man's need, and merged our littleness into God's greatness, and bent our wills to minister to God's will, only then are we allowed to express our own wants for ourselves. 'Give us this day our daily bread,' and here again it is *us*, not *me;* and 'daily bread,' that is, just that provision which enables me to be fitted for my place and work in the kingdom of God, not anything that I should like. And then, because we cannot do God's work unless we are in His favour, therefore, 'Forgive us **our** trespasses,' and that not anyhow, but according to that law by which God deals with us as we deal with our fellow-men, 'Forgive us our trespasses, **as we forgive** them that trespass against us.' And then, because we are frail, and Satan is powerful, 'Bring us not into temptation, but deliver us from the evil one.'

We shall go on to consider somewhat of the rich meaning which lies in these clauses in detail. For the present let us only realize the depth of teaching which lies in the very order of the clauses. Truly, a child may pray that prayer, and the heart of childhood understands it; but it takes the wisest saint to realize anything of the fulness of its meaning.

In this great prayer, then, as much in its general outline as in the particular meaning of the separate clauses, lies the secret of the mind of Christ. In the praying of it consists prayer in His name; and the principle inherent in it is the principle of correspondence.

III

Wbat may we Pray for?

' PRAYER is pleasing to God, that is, the prayer which
is undertaken in the proper manner. He therefore
that desires to be heard should pray wisely, fervently,
humbly, faithfully, perseveringly, confidently. Let
him pray wisely, by which I mean, let him pray for
those things which minister to the divine glory and
the salvation of his neighbours. God is all-powerful,
therefore do not in your prayers prescribe how He shall
act; He is all-wise—therefore do not determine when.
Do not let your prayers break forth heedlessly, but let
them follow the guidance of faith, remembering that
faith has steady regard to the divine word. Those
things, therefore, which God promises absolutely in His
word, those pray for absolutely. Those which He
promises conditionally—for example, temporal things—
those on the same principle pray for conditionally.
Those things which He does not promise at all, those
also you will not pray for at all. God often grants in
His anger what His goodness would deny. Therefore,

21

follow Christ, who fully conforms His will to the will of God.' So wrote the Lutheran Gerhard in his *Holy Meditations*. His advice follows exactly the lines along which our previous considerations have led us. Prayer, we saw, is a form of intelligent correspondence with the revealed will of God. This is the thought we are to continually have in mind when we attempt to answer the often repeated question—what ought we to pray for?

Confining ourselves first of all to the practical aspect of the subject, we may put our answer under four heads.

1. The main object of our prayers must be spiritual things. If we are to pray in the name of Christ, we must seek first the kingdom of God and His righteousness. That is the lesson of the Lord's Prayer. Nor can we omit to notice, that if in one Gospel it is said that our 'Father in heaven will give good things to them that ask him,' the good things are described in another Gospel as 'the Holy Spirit.'[1] For so far as we are Christians in heart, it is upon the possession of the Spirit, with all that that implies, that our desires are concentrated for ourselves and others. For this we can pray with certainty, with the certainty that our persevering prayers for ourselves and others will be heard and answered in proportion to our faith. I say

---

[1] St. Matthew vii. 11 compared with St. Luke xi. 13.

22

answered for ourselves and others : not that God will force the wills of others any more than our own, but that our prayers can secure for them at least the offers of the divine love. This is the region in which our Lord's promise is specially true, 'Verily, I say unto you, whosoever shall say unto this mountain, Be thou taken up and cast into the sea; and shall not doubt in his heart, but shall believe that what he saith cometh to pass ; he shall have it.'[1] Our Lord spoke in a figure, but it was a figure familiar to Jewish hearers. The mountain is the mountain of the world-power which hinders the spiritual spread of the kingdom of God in our own hearts and in the world. This is the moral obstacle which the prayer of the Church, in proportion to its reality and to the unity with which it is offered, shall be able to remove. 'What art thou, O great mountain?' the prophet Zechariah had said of old, 'before Zerubbabel thou shalt become a plain.'[2]

It is then for spiritual things, for the manifestation of spiritual power in the hearts of men, that we are chiefly and primarily to pray. Nor is it easy to over-rate the importance of this right direction of our prayers. True it may be (to take the converse of our Lord's illustration) that even if we ask our Father for a stone He will still give us bread, or for a scorpion, He

---

[1] St. Mark xi. 23. Zech. iv. 7.

will give us fish,[1] but we cannot expect this to be the case where we have the opportunities of better know-ledge; rather, if we pray amiss, let us fear the judg-ment—'God gave them their desire, and sent leanness withal into their souls.'[2]   Nor must we omit to notice, that in controversies raised by materialists about the efficacy of prayer, this characteristic of Christian prayer has generally been left out of sight.   It has been proposed that we should have experiments to test the efficacy of prayer in regard to the long life of kings, or the recovery of the sick.   But nothing can be more certain than this, that prayer is meant to be an exercise of faith which cannot be subjected in our present life to external testing.   And that chiefly because it is in the region of character, in the region where results only fully appear in the eternal world, that prayer is to find its most assured and definite answer.

2. But not all spiritual boons can be asked for. What is asked for must be in accordance with the divine will.   Thus, to ask (as many people do) that they may escape sin, when they will not take reasonable precautions to avoid the occasions of temptation; or to pray for our children, without taking any proper pains in regard to their education; or to pray for spiritual graces, while we refuse the means which the divine will has appointed for their reception; or to pray

---

[1] St. Matt. vii. 9.   [2] Psal. cvi. 15.

for forgiveness for ourselves, when we will neither forgive others nor accept the punishment of our own sins
—these are all examples of the way in which we may
pray for spiritual things lawlessly, or without reference
to the will of God.

3. But it cannot be doubted that we may pray also
for physical things. They must hold the subordinate
place that is given them in the Lord's Prayer, but that
place they must hold—a lesser place than was given
them in the Old Testament, but still a place. A certain supply of physical things, our daily bread, is
necessary to enable us and others to do the work of
God in the world; thus *Give us*, we pray, *our daily
bread*. And that petition can be taken to cover prayers
for health of body, and bettering of social conditions,
and favourable weather. Only we can never pray for
these physical blessings with the same security or
absoluteness as for spiritual. 'Whom the Lord loveth
he chasteneth.' Everything that is included in daily
bread He finally denied to His own Son. To Him He
finally gave no physical deliverance in this life, but left
Him in the extremest sense without physical support.
This is the profound lesson which we learn about
prayer from the prayer of Christ in the Garden of
Gethsemane. So clearly supreme are spiritual over
physical things as objects of prayer, that physical
things can only be prayed for conditionally—'Father,
if it be possible'; and may be denied even to the well-

beloved, even as the cup did not pass from Christ without His drinking it. Still, granted this, there are a great number of physical things which, as far as the Christian in this world can see, it would be good for him or others to have, such as health, supply of food, weather, and so on. In regard to these we should put up real petitions, which, if accompanied with a willingness to see them not granted, or prefaced by 'Not my will, but thine be done,' should still be prayers which expect an answer from the divine love. It is the great function of the spiritual man to see to it, that within that region where the human will has its exercise, spiritual motives and forces shall have their full sway in determining events; and for all we know the divine government of the world may, for the testing of our faith, have left a real function for prayer to fulfil in reinforcing the springs of vitality in sick men, and even in ordering, within certain limits, the character of the weather.

4. I say, 'for all we know,' and I am looking at the matter now practically, not metaphysically. How do we know the divine will? We know it from the revelation in conscience and through Christ. We know it also in the order of the physical world. Science has recently been disclosing increasingly what the order of the physical world is, what its laws are. Like the revealed laws of the spiritual kingdom, the known physical laws are limits to prayer. No doubt from

time to time prophets and righteous men have been specially inspired to pray for miracles. With such exceptional inspirations we are not now concerned. Ordinarily, a known law of the physical world is a declaration of the will of God. So far, therefore, as the physical laws of the world are known, so far as scientific men can prophesy what will happen in accordance with these laws, to pray against them would be to pray against God. But there is a region into which human prescience cannot penetrate. We know indeed that it belongs to the fixed order of nature that we should not have tropical weather in a temperate climate, but within limits there is no fixed order in the sequence of different kinds of weather which is known to us. It is certainly true that men, by planting or destroying trees, can in lapse of time modify weather. Nor can it be said to be certain, from a scientific point of view, that the action of free will by means of prayer may not have a similar power within similar limits to modify the weather—conceivably through the mediation of invisible spiritual forces or persons, as to which we know nothing. We doubt very much whether those scientific men who will be most peremptory in denying this, will be prepared to admit that there is such a thing at all as a real freedom within certain restricted limits, assigned to human wills in ordering the course of physical events; or that we can, by the exercise of our free wills, make the course of events different from what it otherwise would have been. Granted there is this freedom, for example, to modify weather by planting trees or accumulating waters, there can be no scientific demonstration that prayer may not have a similar restricted but real influence.

Christians will certainly go on trustfully commending their wishes about the weather to their heavenly Father's attention, as well as the health of their friends, until science has got a power, altogether different from what it now wields, of predicting future events in these districts of experience. For only such power of prediction would make it apparent that in these, as in the vaster physical movements, events are simply determined in accordance with physical laws, without any reference to moral or spiritual causes. And if this seems already certain to men of physical science, on the other hand, the spiritual experience of men of prayer has in all ages given them great encouragement in praying for the recovery of their friends and for seasonable weather.

In this paper I have trespassed very slightly on the speculative ground, and my main object was to give a practical answer to the question, what are the proper objects of prayer? To deal at length with the philosophic or scientific problem would require more space than is at present at my command, and more knowledge. But the broad position of the Christian is this, and in occupying it he stands on the strongest ground—It is the business of the spiritual man to assert, within certain limits, the mastery of the human spirit in accordance with the divine will over its material surroundings. It does this mainly through the strengthening of character. It does it in part through altering external conditions. How far the power allowed to the human spirit extends into the material world cannot be certainly said, but limits can only be assigned to it with certainty at that point where science can prove the importance of human freedom by predictions of the course of events on a basis purely physical ; and the power of prayer may be commensurate with the power of the human spirit. If we can alter circumstances by willing and working, we may alter them also by willing and praying. But we must not conclude this discussion without repeating that the main objects of Christian prayer are spiritual things. Only in regard to these can prayer rise with the confident expectation of being answered. .

©ur father whicb art in beaven

OUR Lord, as was said above, did not give us mere abstract principles of prayer, but something much more intelligible—an example or pattern of prayer. And this, which we call 'The Lord's Prayer,' is not so much one prayer among many, as for Christians the type in which all their praying is to be moulded, the form which is to express each petition they wish to offer, the test of whether indeed it is a permissible petition at all. We proceed then to reflect upon its several clauses.

Our Father which art in heaven.

We begin by solemnly invoking God under His character as a Father. To approach God as our Father was indeed in apostolic times understood to be the great and distinctive privilege of Christians. 'God hath sent forth the Spirit of his Son into our hearts, crying, *Abba, Father.'* [1] And indeed it requires but little thought to perceive that it makes the whole difference

---

[1] 1 Gal. iv. 6.

in prayer whether we in fact realize that God is our common Father. What we ask of men, and the expectation with which we ask it, depends on what we think of them. With what difference in our hopes do we ask for some sacrifice or some kindness of different people! With what fulness of hope ought we to present ourselves with our requests before God, whom we believe in as Father. God's Fatherhood means that He has brought us into being. The responsibility for bringing other lives into existence rests indeed in large measure on earthly parents. But behind all, it rests on God our Creator. God, who has created us, because He is also our Father, is bound to care for each of His creatures; bound to make the best of each. Not indeed that He can exempt them from the moral discipline which belongs to rational and free beings, or can exempt them from the consequences of it. God, we may well say, *cannot* prevent us experiencing the consequences, and even the eternal consequences, of our own moral wilfulness. But, consistently with the laws of our being, He can make the best of us. And this we can confidently entreat of Him to do for each. None is forgotten in His sight. None is under-rated. There is no forgetfulness and no favouritism. There is discipline for all, but contempt for none. The God whom we approach is the Father of all, and accepts—nay, desires to have pressed upon Him in prayer—the responsibility of His Fatherhood.

And we further qualify His Fatherhood by the addition to '*Our Father*' of the words '*which art in heaven.*' No doubt this expression recalls a time when men thought of the sky as a vault not so very far above their heads, and of God, or gods, as residing just beyond the vault, as it were on the upper storey of the universal house. Now in our scientific age we know that there is no ceiling over our heads, and no possibility of locating God somewhere above. But none the less we cannot help thinking and talking in the old figures; and we know what 'lift up your hearts' means as well as our less scientific forefathers. Indeed, long before the age of science, long before the time of our Lord, God's residence in heaven had come to have a moral meaning attached to it. His spiritual omnipresence was asserted by psalmists and prophets, and the true meaning of His heavenliness proclaimed. 'As the heavens are higher than the earth, so are my ways higher than your ways, and my thoughts than your thoughts.'[1] The idea then that we are intended to attach to God's *heavenly* Fatherhood is, that He is infinitely raised above us in the height of His holiness and the largeness of His wisdom. To call God our Father in heaven, is to lift up our minds in awful reverence above all the narrowness, short-sightedness, shallowness, and defilement of earth, and to remember

---

[1] Isa. lv. 9.

that the best we can think or imagine or hope is but a feeble image of the largeness, the resourcefulness, the richness, the holiness of the mind of God. 'God is in heaven, and thou upon earth; therefore let thy words be few.'[1] God is farther from us in the loftiness of His revealed character than ever He seemed to be to Greeks or Romans, who fashioned Him after their own likeness in temper and lusts. But, on the other hand, He is infinitely nearer to us in the condescension of His love. It is only sin that kept earth, the abode of men, apart from heaven, the abode of God. Now the 'kingdom of heaven' or 'of God' is 'come'; it is 'within us,' or among us. Our 'citizenship is in heaven.' The Christian institutions are 'heavenly things.' We are made to sit 'in heavenly places in Christ.'[2] All this language describes the intimate closeness of union which in Christ has been granted us with the heavenly God. Thus in appealing to 'our Father which is in heaven' we are appealing to one who is 'closer than breathing' and 'nearer than hands and feet,' to whom the slightest motion of the heart and will is audible. How is it, then, that so many people still in their spiritual imagination think of God in heaven as if He were far off, so that it needed some great effort to penetrate to His abode?

[1] Eccl. v. 2.

[2] St. Matt. xii. 28 ; St. Luke xvii. 21 ; Phil. iii. 20 ; Heb. ix. 23 ; Eph. i. 3.

Hallowed be Thy Name.

The name of God means the revelation of God, or rather God as He makes Himself known to men ; and we may say, that human history is in one aspect the record of the way in which God has gradually spelt out His name among men, or suffered them to spell it out. Something of that name is discovered in the aspect and processes of nature ; something again is audible in the whispered suggestions and threatenings of conscience ; some elements of it have become apparent to the founders of the different religions of the world ; but nowhere is the gradual process of discovery so distinct as among the Jews. At the bottom of the Old Testament revelation the personality and personal dealings of God are indeed strongly emphasized, but the conceptions of His infinitude, His holiness, His spirituality, leave still very much to be gained. That His holiness is moral, not ceremonial, reveals itself to prophet after prophet. His love is discovered to a Hosea, His impartiality to an Ezekiel, His sympathy with the sorrows of His people to an Isaiah. And all that was disclosed to prophets was deepened in His revelation by the Son, through whom the name of God is finally spelt out as the name of the Father, the Son, and the Holy Ghost, with all the moral significance attaching to each of the elements of this threefold name.

In the Lord's Prayer the place of primary importance is given to the petition that God's revelation of Himself may be held in honour, " Hallowed be thy Name." The matter of first and dominant importance is, that men should believe and hold what is true about the being and character of God, and believing aright, should let their belief be expressed in the reverence of their lives.

It may be said of the pagan religions—not without qualification, but generally—that the character ascribed to God in them is the simple reflection of the character of His worshippers. The most powerful modern expression of this lower anthropomorphism, this fashioning of gods after the image of men, is to be found in Browning's poem of *Caliban upon Setebos*. Poor savage Caliban is there represented as ascribing all his own arbitrariness and fitfulness to Setebos his god. This is an universal tendency; but in the Bible we have the record of the counter process, which, if it were going on everywhere in a measure, was nowhere enacted as among the Jews—the process of God impressing Himself as He truly is on the hearts and intellects of His people. True it is that the self-revelation of God at its highest verifies the belief in a special kinship of man to God. Man at his best recognizes his own best self infinitely glorified in the character of God as manifested in Christ. Still, here is a revelation of God to man, not a fashioning of God after man's ideas; and the result is, that it lays on men a strong and searching claim to re-model their own natures, that they may become truly in the divine image. To believe in God as He is indeed, is to recognize our need to be born again and fashioned anew.

How is it that some people are so shallow-minded as to suppose that it makes no difference what a man believes about God? The contrary lies written in the record of history. For, however inconsistent are men's beliefs and practices, if you look at individual men at a particular moment, yet if you look at human nature in its long reaches and over its broad surfaces, it appears that men's conduct has depended on what they think about God. The civilizations which have grown up under the influence of Jewish, Greek, Mohammedan, Buddhist, and Christian beliefs about God, have been morally different civilizations. And the necessary connection between the intelligence and the will in man makes it necessary that belief should, in the long run, mould behaviour.

Hallowed be God's name then! Let Christians believe with all their hearts in the Father, Son, and Holy Ghost—one God; and believing, have the courage to profess their belief, and let it mould their public conduct and their private lives. It is probably quite true, in fact mathematically true, that 'there lives more faith in honest doubt than in half the creeds,' for half the creeds, that is, the beliefs of half the believers, are little more than formalisms, and of little moral value; whereas honest doubts, the sincere seekings of the perplexed hearts from whom God's face is hidden, have a great deal of moral value, and are undoubtedly on the way to final light. But it does not therefore follow, nor is it true, that 'there lives more faith,' or more value, in doubts in general than in sincere creeds. Indeed, quite the opposite is the case; and no one who knows anything of current society can fail to perceive that a great deal which passes for religious doubt proceeds from little but want of moral effort, and worldliness, and very often lack of moral courage. Doubt, however inevitable in some cases, need not be a normal condition of mind. Renan used cynically to remark, that very few people have the qualifications for being sceptics. And if we want to play our part as men and Christians in the world, we should do our best to believe simply, and to confess loyally in worship and in conduct the faith which we believe. How vast a part of what is worst in modern society is due to lack of moral courage! How deep the truth in our Lord's question—'How can ye believe which seek glory one of another, and the glory which cometh of the only God ye seek not?'

Let us then learn to pray *Hallowed be Thy Name*, and indeed to give it the dominant and leading place in all our prayers. God has revealed Himself. If under a veil, He can yet be known by us, and we pray that the infinite benefit of this revelation of Himself may be realized and accepted by all men. *Hallowed be Thy Name by being believed.* And believing on God in their hearts, we pray that men may not be ashamed of their best selves, but may confess Him in their lives, and pay to Him the outward reverence which is reasonable from men to God. *Hallowed be Thy Name by frank outward confession.* And we pray that the public worship of the Church may be a worship in spirit and in truth, a worship worthy of its great object; for we remember the sane words of Hooker—'Duties of religion performed by whole societies of men ought to have in them a sensible excellency correspondent to the majesty of Him whom we worship.' *Hallowed be Thy Name by glorious and spiritual worship.* Lastly, we pray that men may hallow the name of God in their own private lives, and live worthily of that holy name in that 'holiness without which no man shall see the Lord.' *Hallowed be Thy Name in the continual sanctification of the lives of Christians,* that they may indeed be, in the Son and through the Spirit, a holy priesthood to God, even the Father.

V

Thy Kingdom come . . . as in Heaven so on Earth

WHAT is a kingdom? It is a society of men living in an orderly manner a common life under one head or ruler. The kingdom of God is this, but more. For human rule is over men only, speaking generally; the rule of God is over all created things whatever. Thus the kingdom of God is an orderly constitution of all things visible and invisible, inanimate, animate and spiritual, each in its own place fulfilling the divine will.

A kingdom is not a kingdom unless there is order. A perfect kingdom involves perfect order. Thus the idea of order in nature and in the world as a whole was postulated by religion, from the point of view of the kingdom of God, long before it was postulated by science. God, says the Psalmist, has given to all the parts of nature 'a law which shall not be broken.' The divine Wisdom, says the later Solomon, ' reacheth from one end of the world to the other with full strength, and ordereth all things graciously.'[1] But as soon as ever we have begun to think of the world as a divine kingdom with a divine order, the question at once arises, is this order perfect and complete? And the prompt answer is, No. Without doing violence to our moral conscience, it is impossible to treat wickedness, cruelty, falsehood, as a part of a divine order or the keeping of a divine command. Thus we are landed in the position of St. John. Sin is lawlessness.[2] St. John's expression in the Greek language means exactly that sin and lawlessness are coincident. Nowhere in the world is there disorder till you come to the wilfulness or sin of spiritual beings, and sin does not begin till wilfulness or lawlessness begins. This is the fundamental Christian doctrine of sin. Sin is not imperfection merely, the imperfection of undeveloped natures, which it only requires time to develop more perfectly. Sin, again, is not ignorance which it requires only right knowledge to remove. Imperfection and ignorance indeed are realities and have to be reckoned with; but the wilfulness of spiritual beings using their freedom to rebel against God, and so spoiling the divine order in the world down to the depth to which their power and activity extend—this and this only is sin. This rebellion of free spirits has its effects on the sinning individual, and its results are also transmitted as a long

---

[1] Wisdom viii. 1 (R. V.).   [2] 1 John iii. 4. (R. V.).

heritage of misery and disorder to those who come after. This idea of sin was in a measure, by the help of their consciences, arrived at by thinkers outside the revelation of the Old and New Covenant. There is, for example, a splendid expression of sin as spoiling the divine order of the world in that hymn to Zeus of the stoic Cleanthes, from which St. Paul at Athens quoted the expression, 'For we are also the offspring of God.' 'Nothing,' cries Cleanthes, 'takes place on earth apart from Thee, nor in the heaven above, nor in the deep, except the things which bad men do in their senselessness, . . . who neither perceive nor listen to the common law of God.' But the doctrine received its most authoritative declaration in the New Testament. Throughout that volume man is treated as a being involved in sin, who needs therefore not only development and enlightenment, but also redemption. And the beginning of this mystery of sin is not found in the human will; for broad - and deep as has been the development of sin among men, there is still beyond men an order of rebel wills about whom we know little, but of whose existence and activity we are assured, the devil and his angels, to whose activity man's seduction is traced, and who are represented as being at work not in man only, but in nature.

Now all this is taken for granted when we pray 'Thy kingdom come.' The necessity for this prayer arises only because the rule of God in the world has been—

not indeed banished, but obscured. So that from the point of view of sinful, alienated man, the kingdom of God, His manifested rule, must be treated as an absent thing to be desired and invoked.

But it may be said, Has not that kingdom come? Is it not the kingdom of Christ? Was it not to establish or re-establish it that Christ came? Quite true. Our Lord taught us that it came with His coming, and at the same time He taught His disciples to pray for it as a thing not yet come. Here is a contradiction in words such as our Lord never shrank from, because the apparent contradiction challenges thought and reveals a deeper meaning underneath.

The kingdom of God or of Heaven has come. For our Lord established a Church, or visible society, which He identified with the kingdom. His parables of the drag-net that gathered of every kind of fish (St. Matt. xiii. 47), and of the field of wheat amidst which tares are sown by an enemy (St. Matt. xiii. 24), both represent the kingdom of God as a visible institution or society in which the good and evil are mixed together. They identify, in fact, the kingdom of God with the visible Church. Again, when our Lord said that John the Baptist, though he was the greatest of those born of woman, was yet, by his very position, outside the kingdom of God,[1] so that the little ones in the kingdom have higher privileges than he, He identifies the

[1] St. Matt. xi. 11.

kingdom of God with the society He was founding. The Church, then, is the kingdom of God, or the kingdom of Heaven, because it is an organized society of men, in which Christ is the Head and King, in which His will is known and obeyed, and in which visible ceremonies and outward realities are interpenetrated with the life of heaven. It was pointed out in the last paper, how the language of the New Testament continually supposes that to be in the Church is to be among the heavenly things or in the heavenly places. Thus the Church is, in virtue of the spiritual realities that it enshrines, truly and really the kingdom of God. But it is so within limitations; for in the first place, if the power of the kingdom is at work within the Church, it is so secretly; the kingdom is not manifested openly before man's eyes. It requires faith to recognize it and see it. And in the next place, the power is only felt in a comparatively narrow region, within the limits of a society which does not represent the whole of mankind, still less the whole of the universe. Thus, if from the point of view of the spiritual forces that are at work in her, the Church *is* the kingdom, from another and larger point of view the Church *represents* the kingdom within a certain area of time and place, and prepares for the larger and fuller representation of the empire of God in the universe.

When we pray, then, 'Thy kingdom come,' we are praying for the spread of the Church, for all that promotes her spiritual well-being and influence, for the believing of her message, for the acceptance of the grace which she is permitted to dispense, for the practice of her discipline among those who are at present neglecting it, and in the world of heathendom where men have not yet learnt the meaning of the sacred name. All that a Churchman can desire in the Church and for the Church is contained in the prayer, 'Thy kingdom come.' But also, and perhaps more prominently, it is a prayer for the second coming of Christ, that is, the manifest and open exhibition of His empire, not only over and in the Church, but in the whole universe.

Let us learn to pray, then, ' Thy kingdom come,' over our own lawless and rebellious thoughts, desires, and passions ; and in the world outside us, wherever a selfish luxury and sensuality, or jealousy, selfishness and cruelty, or pride and wilfulness and contempt of the truth prevail. And, to speak plainly, this is almost every-where, in our domestic life and commerce and politics, very often in religion. Moreover, we cannot pray for the kingdom unless we are prepared to fight for it also. We all love peace and smoothness, but we forget that if peace is the end of Christ's rule, war is the method by which it is to be won. ' I came not to send peace on earth, but a sword.' That is what we do so terribly forget. This duty of fighting for the kingdom of God, for the cause of truth and righteousness and meekness, belongs to all Christians : not to the clergy, but to the

Christians. We shall make no palpable way in the world at all till we have learnt that the Church does not consist of the clergy, but that every baptized member of the body of Christ is pledged to be a fighter for the truth and the morality of the kingdom in every single department of his life. This is not comfortable doctrine at all, yet it is the doctrine we want. And Established Churches need more particularly to recollect, that to be doing this is the only sort of Church defence against the judgments of God that has any real value whatever. Thy kingdom come, then, O God, as in heaven so on earth!

For the phrase, 'as in heaven so on earth,' applies in all probability not only to the clause after which it occurs about the divine will, but also to the two earlier ones—Hallowed be Thy Name, as in heaven so on earth; Thy kingdom come, as in heaven so on earth. Let that day come when the supremacy of the Lord and His Christ shall be an open and acknowledged thing, which may be to some anguish unutterable, but can be to none deniable. Meanwhile, let the kings of the earth stand up, and the rulers take council together against the Lord and against His Anointed ; but we at least will not be frightened. He that dwelleth in heaven shall laugh them to scorn, and on the overthrow of all rebellious enterprises and long-drawn-out antagonisms open and secret, the kingdoms of the world shall become the kingdom of the Lord and of His Christ.

45

VI

Thy will be done, as in Heaven so on Earth

PAUL BOURGET, the well-known French novelist and
man of letters, went three years ago for a visit to
America. What impressed him there, with a force
which appears continually in the fascinating account of
his expedition which he has given in *Outre-mer*, was
the omnipresent spirit of enterprise. Everywhere in
men and women he met with a vigorous and powerful
will—a will bent on being successful, bent on seizing the
exact situation under which present effectiveness was
most possible. This vigorous will, this enterprise, is,
as we all proudly recognize, the mark of the Anglo-
Saxon race; but then, as we know it, this vigorous will
has a way of showing itself in the form of vigorous
competition. We walk down the streets of our towns,
and watch one tradesman contending against another
in a self-advertisement, to say the least of it, not over-
scrupulous about truth, each using all his cleverness to
under-sell and make life impossible for the other. And

what we see among individuals appears also among classes. If Labour organizes itself, it is against Capital. If Capital combines, it is to offer more effective resistance to the pressure of a strong Trades Union. The area enlarges itself, but its spirit is still the same. In France, in Germany, in England, in Russia, in Italy a vast expenditure is going on to arm every nation against every other. And the same competition is at least as apparent in the race for Africa, or the jealous watching of one nation by another, lest any should get an advantage over the others in the dismemberment of the Turkish Empire. Nor is this spirit less apparent in the matter of religion. The assertion of the individual will, the determination to work a successful enterprise, in a word, the spirit of competition, has intruded itself there. It has split the Christian Church into an infinite number of sects; and it is only too lamentably apparent, that a large proportion of what is called religious energy is occupied, not in combating sin and falsehood, but in pressing against one another the claims of different religious bodies. Enterprise, energy, will, ambition, these are marks then of the human race, and especially the Anglo-Saxon race, and the form in which they show themselves is a universal and unlimited competition.

Now there is no doubt at all that, if we are to make the best of ourselves, we must kindle to the very uttermost in all men the will to be, the will to realize all that is in them; nay, more, we must kindle even the appetite for enjoyment, for after all enjoyment is, as Aristotle says, the crown and accompaniment of every completed activity, and to develop our faculties is in the long run to secure the most permanent and deepest enjoyment. And it is also no doubt true, that this will to realize ourselves carries us far off from one another and makes us different. To work at our best is to work with the greatest amount of individual difference. We work best when we are least restrained by the cramping necessity of being like some one else. The development of individuality then means the development of differences, means a world full of strong and dissimilar modes of operation. Then the question arises, must strong and unlike individualities be necessarily in antagonism? Can there be no vigour except competitive vigour, and no development of unlikeness that is not also a development of hostility? Now it is to this question that the better conscience of mankind, wearied with the waste of life which unlimited competition produces, is giving an emphatic No. Everywhere men of all sorts are asking, how can we introduce a spirit of co-operation to supplant or to modify the spirit of competition? Thus we are aiming at Boards of Conciliation between Capital and Labour, which shall represent to each party that their separate interests lie not only in the strong organization of each, but also in the recognition of a common interest over both. There is more real hope than at any previous time of the establishment of a system of arbitration, at least between the two great and predominantly Anglo-Saxon nations. Once again, when people see some necessity of life, such as water, manipulated not always in the interests of the consumer, to the profit of a body of shareholders in a water company, they are asking themselves, why should not the municipality (everywhere, as has already been done in some places) take the place of the private company, and let the water be manipulated in the interests of all? Tardily, moreover, —lamentably tardily, but still we hope with greater promise of effectiveness—the same class of questions is being asked in the region of religion, and the anti-Christian spectacle of rival and competing sects is at least becoming a burden on the consciences of a greater number of people. Thus everywhere the old Christian idea of the body corporate is on the way to a revival. The body represents unity in diversity; it results from the development of the most marked variety of function in individual limbs, the most marked variety of differences in their methods of working, but all dominated by one common interest—not competing, but co-operating. 'For the body is one and hath many members, and all the members of the body, being many, are one body. If the foot shall say, because I am not the hand I am not of the body, it is not therefore not of the body; and if the ear shall say, because I am not the

49   E

eye I am not of the body, it is not therefore not of the
body. If the whole body were an eye where were the
hearing? If the whole were hearing, where were the
smelling? But now they are many members, but one
body; and the eye cannot say to the hand I have no
need of thee, or again, the head to the feet I have no
need of you. Nay, much rather, those members of the
body which seem to be more feeble are necessary; and
those parts of the body which we think to be less
honourable, on these we put on (in the way of dress)
more abundant honour, and our uncomely parts have
more abundant comeliness; whereas our comely parts
have no need. But God tempered the body together,
giving more abundant honour to the parts which
lacked; that there should be no schism in the body,
but that the members should have the same care one
for another, and where one member suffers all the
members suffer with it, and where one member is
honoured all the members rejoice with it.'

This is the divine ideal of the Universe, that each
creature—inanimate, animate, rational—should find its
joy in realizing its own function, that is, in being the
thing it is meant to be, in experiencing the joy proper
to itself, and in seeing all the other creatures realizing
all their separate functions, while all together contribute
to a common end. No doubt sacrifice, the sacrifice of
one to the other, is more or less knit up into the heart
of this process. But God does not shrink from requiring

sacrifice. No doubt gradation is inseparable from combination, and one must rejoice to be higher, and another rejoice to be lower. But God has no sympathy with the desire to excel each the other for vain-glory's sake. When Dante in Paradise expected to find those in its lowest places deploring that they were not higher, he was reproved for introducing an idea of competition and jealousy altogether subversive of the life of heaven.

'E la sua voluntade è nostra pace.'

'God's will is our peace,' was the reply of the questioned spirit. That is the law of heaven, the law of archangels and angels and just men made perfect, each joyfully occupying his own place and fulfilling his own function —each obeying, and in obedience free; free, because he finds in obedience his essential good. And we pray, like Richard Hooker on his death-bed, that this law of heaven may become the law of earth—to the overthrow of the principle of mere self-assertion and competition, Thy will be done, as in heaven so on earth.

It was for the realizing of this ideal that the Church was divinely created. Its maxim is, let each man look not to his own things only, but also to the things of others; and its ideal has been again and again realized, at least, in great and effective measure. In the early Church, in days when it cost men much to become Christians, we have a spectacle of happy co-operation, the like of which the world has never seen equalled. And, again and again, when the spirit of worldliness and competition has corrupted the Church at large, earnest men have gathered themselves together and formed fresh centres of unselfish life, centres of co-operation. Such were the religious orders, especially in the West, both of men and women; such was the co-operative family life among the Moravians; such is to be found in the heart of every Christian parish or enterprise where the Spirit of God is at work. Everywhere there are men and women taxing all their energies in work, for their own happiness, no doubt, but also for the common good—the good of the whole body which is the glory of God, for 'the glory of God is the living man.' But, alas! the measure in which we have realized our ideal is nothing compared with the boundlessness of our failure hitherto. In its own proper sphere the Church has allowed the spirit of the world to enter into her, and she has altogether failed to realize her catholicity by making her power felt in politics and in commerce. Once again we are waking to our duty. Once again we pray with more earnestness, that the idea of service like Christ's co-operative service may take the place of selfish ambition and wasteful competition, Thy will be done, as in heaven so on earth.

II

The prayer is a prayer against selfishness; it is equally a prayer against sloth. No doubt, in the world, and especially in our Anglo-Saxon world, there is a great deal of energy, but side by side with it there is a vast deal of sloth. Think of it! The sloth of intellect; the sloth which seems to make men unwilling, for all our increasing education, to read anything longer than a paragraph in a newspaper with a sensational headline and perhaps a picture. The sloth of intellect which, in religious things, is terrified by the appearance of doubt and difficulty, and imagines that the only sign of excellence in a religion is to be found in that clearness of authoritative dogma which will dispense the individual from the trouble of thinking. Or again, sluggishness in prayer, how widespread it is—how paralyzing to one of the richest of human activities! Or, once more, what sloth there is with regard to the imagination—what a lack of will to regulate effectively this powerful human faculty! Thus, instead of its being a storehouse of dominant ideas, inspiring, consecrating, and ruling life, it becomes the mere passive slave of every unclean spectacle, of every foolish suggestion, of every profitless day-dream. Once more, what sluggishness of heart there is! Where true love is kindled every faculty brightens; but where the heart is dead or cold, what paralysis ensues of the faculties of thinking, and sympathizing, and contriving, and willing!

'Thy will be done,' then, is a prayer against sloth.

> 'It is the will sends the renewing nerve
> Through flaccid flesh, that faints before the time'—

it is the will; the human will, but most effectively the human will possessed by the divine will, and following along with it, as with Jesus of Nazareth, in whole-hearted and unconditional obedience to the mind of God.

Let our imaginations rest, then, on the burning love, the thrilling knowledge of those dimly known spiritual beings, archangels and angels; on the keen joy of vision which has been obtained by the spirits of just men made perfect. And let us pray that, with a like effect-iveness, now in our days of darkness and difficulty, an effectiveness to be crowned at last with a like reward, God's will may be done, as in heaven so on earth.

And who can tell what an utterly different place the world would look, if those who do intend to be sincere Christians would realize the duty of vigorous and effective willing, vigorous and effective co-operation, to bring about the kingdom of God in this world! The Christian religion is a religion of comfort, and 'comfort' (*confortare*), with its Greek original, means first of all to make strong or to encourage. Religion is to put heart and courage into us, both to work and to pray, to co-operate according to the divine will both for the overthrow of the kingdom of darkness and the establishment of the kingdom of God. 'Thy will be done in earth as it is in heaven.'

VII

Give us this Day our Daily Bread

I

THE first point to notice in this clause of the Lord's Prayer is its moderation. In the prayer which is prompted by our natural instinct we ask for everything we happen to want: we put ourselves first; we are immoderate in our desires; we seek to bend the divine will to our own wishes. In all these respects, as has been already noticed, the Lord's Prayer puts human instinct under the strongest check. This prayer for the supply of our own needs is not allowed to be uttered till it has been postponed to prayer for the honouring of the divine name, the coming of the divine kingdom, and the doing of the divine will; and till, in all these respects, the law of heaven has been taken for the law of human conduct. It is only to state the same fact in other words, to call attention to the suppression of individualism which lies in the very words 'us' and 'our,' words which prevent us praying for anything for ourselves which we cannot equally request for the

56

whole society; and, once more, the same principle finds expression in the word 'bread.' It is 'bread,' and not anything we may happen to like, that we are allowed to pray for. This, then, is the prayer of the Christian Church, the prayer which the existing Christian Church here in England to-day is continually repeating. Yet it certainly is not an exaggeration to say, that though there are among us always true Christians praying this prayer in spirit as well as in letter, yet a vast number of repetitions of the Lord's Prayer must be blank hypocrisy; for it is hypocrisy if the prayer of our lips is a quite different thing from the prayer of our hearts. Yet the prayer of our heart is expressed in what we actually show ourselves to want and to expect in our ordinary life. Listen, then, to two praying Christians, who are discussing the marriage of their son and daughter, and in the process are making a number of assumptions as to what is the minimum of wealth on which life can be reasonably conducted. Look at that other person furnishing a house, or providing for a dinner-party. Think, in short, of all the things which in ordinary conversation Christians are ready to say 'they can't do without.' Think of the money spent in a single rich household on a single article of luxury like champagne, or a single article of dress. Now, things which are the actual wants of actual people are the prayers of their hearts. And if they cannot possibly be expressed in a petition for daily bread, then I fear, their saying of the Lord's Prayer. is nothing else than a more or less conscious hypocrisy.

What, then, can daily bread be explained to mean? Surely it is all that is necessary for us to make the best of our faculties. It is nourishment; and everything may fairly be called nourishment which can be said to fertilize and liberate the energies of human nature, instead of cloying and clogging them. Once grant this, and it is obvious that very different things are meant by 'bread' to different people. There is hardly any luxury which has not its use to stimulate this or that nature, or to meet this or that exceptional need. The question whether this or that article of diet or comfort can be used under the head of 'daily bread,' can be answered only by answering the question—Do I work the better for it and pray the better for it? And in answering this question there are two facts, closely allied, which have to be kept in mind. The first is, that comforts very soon reach the point where they begin to clog instead of liberating human energies. A venerable statesman has been often heard to remark, that the things people say they 'can't do without' are like the pieces of thread with which the Liliputians bound Gulliver. Each of them could be snapt by itself, but taken together they bound him more tightly than strong cords. Nobody, therefore, can find out what he really needs for his work without constantly testing himself in giving up things. No one can consider a

58

number of well-to-do Englishmen without perceiving that they are materialized; that is, that the supply of food and drink and comfort generally dulls their intellectual and still more their spiritual powers. In other words, the spirit in them is the slave of the flesh. Here, then, comes in view the second fact. Fasting has been historically a principle of Christianity, and was so in Apostolic Christianity. Rightly stated, the principle of fasting is but the recognition that the flesh has in ordinary human life got the upper hand of the spirit, and that it is time for the spirit to take revenges upon the flesh, and to assert its mastery. Fasting, like every other principle, must have its methods and its rules and its order, or it will fail to take effect; but I am concerned only now with the principle, and it is this—The Christian will, from time to time, deliberately deny himself in lawful comforts, and nourishments of the body, in order to assert spiritual vitality; in order to find out what he can do without; in order to maintain the principle that 'man doth not live by bread alone, but by every word that proceedeth out of the mouth of God.'

Bread, then, is the nourishment necessary to make the body an effective instrument for fulfilling the spiritual purpose of our life, or, in other words, to enable us to make the best of ourselves. And what his 'bread' ought to consist of the individual can never find out unless he has steadily in view the encroaching tendency of the flesh; unless he is prepared, on the one hand, to make courageous trials in ‘doing without,’ and on the other hand is prepared thankfully to accept anything in the way of holiday, or rest, or food, or drink, or comfort, which reasonable experience shows to be necessary to keep him in efficiency, and make him vigorous in profitable industry and in communion with God. The body is to be a serviceable instrument, and it is a good creation of God. It is to be the instrument and not the master, but it is to be kept as an efficient instrument, and not maltreated any more than any other of the creatures of God.

Now when we reflect, we cannot fail to see that, if over any large area of Christian society the principles embodied in this prayer were really respected, there would be plenty of God's gifts for every one's need. Granted a society in which men would really pray ‘Thy will be done on earth,’ and ‘ Give us this day our daily bread,’ and would live with even tolerable consistency in accordance with their prayer,—in that society would be found a human life which, if it did not perfectly realize the kingdom of God on earth, would at least be a foretaste and convincing prophecy of it. It is a good thing to take a walk and meditate upon such a proposition. It fixes in our minds this conclusion—the misery of the world is manufactured by man. Certainly—

> ‘To the flame that ruineth mankind,
> Man gives the matter, or at least gives wind.’

II

Oddly enough, in the simple language of this prayer appears one of the most difficult words in the New Testament. The word translated *daily* probably means bread '*for the coming day.*' It has been recently suggested, that its occurrence side by side with 'to-day' is due to the very early use of this prayer by Christians both morning and evening : that in the morning they said, 'Give us our bread to-day,' and in the evening, 'Give us our bread for to-morrow.' The suggestion puts us at least on the right line of thought. The prayer is the prayer of those who are content to depend from day to day in trustfulness on their Father's love. When our Lord in the Sermon on the Mount forbade us to be anxious about food or drink or clothing, what He forbade was anxiety, not providence. The birds of the air and the flowers of the field, to which He looked for examples, all in their unconscious way make provision. From the time the seed is sown provision is being made for the growth, and the flowering, and the fruitage, which are each in turn to come. When the birds build their nests they are making provision for the future of themselves and their race. But they do it all without any anxiety. They do each day the work of the day, and expect each day the supplies of the day. Now granted a like providence, a like industrious work-fulness, and the prayerful trust in God which is the spiritual counterpart of their unanxious happiness, and who can doubt that in ninety-nine cases out of a hundred the prayer, ' Give us this day our daily bread,' would be found to be answered. In other words, the misery of the world, the destitution which we continually hear of, is due either to want of reasonable provision, or to idleness, luxury, and vice, or to prayerless, thankless want of trust. The prayer, ' Give us to-day our daily bread,' is the prayer of men who are at once thinking and believing and working.

III

I said the word translated *daily* means properly the bread *'for to-morrow.'* But in old days it was very generally translated ' super-substantial ' — that is to say, the bread that is higher than material—or in other words, spiritual bread, ' the bread of life.' So the prayer became associated with the service of the Eucharist, with the continual feeding on the Bread of Life, which is Jesus Christ, very God and very man. Now, the translation was no doubt wrong. The prayer is one for physical and not spiritual nourishment. But yet to the Christian it can never be without the deepest significance, that the bread of the Spirit is given us in common bread; that the original Eucharist was side by side with the love-feast, the highest things in closest connection with the most ordinary. Alas! the abuses of the Corinthian Church separated the Eucharist and the love-feast wide apart. Alas! that it should have been necessary to do so. But though it be necessary, as necessary it is, the principle must never be forgotten which is embodied in the fact, that it is common bread which is made to become to us the body of Christ; and that the communication to us of Christ's own being, the communion of His body and blood, was made on the occasion and under the forms of a fraternal meal. Thus common eating and drinking are touched for the Christian with a sacramental meaning; and the sharing the good things which God provides for our nourishment is one chief means of realizing the unity of the Christian body which is in the one Spirit. There is no real Christian meal which ought not to be consecrated with the thought of unity with Christ, and lifted by the sense of brotherhood and co-operation. 'Give us this day our daily bread,' the bread for the body, and through the bread for the body that life of the soul also which is communion with God and with our brother men.

So let us pray 'Give us this day our daily bread.' *Us !* it is the *we* of each household; the *we* of each parish, each town, in which all classes are mingled together; it is the *we* also of the whole Christian family. Our thoughts when we pray this prayer ought sometimes to go out to that unhappy community of Armenians recently butchered and hunted in their mountain homes, and massacred in thousands in the streets of Constantinople, and still subject to continual outrages and murders and forced conversions, while Christian Europe looks on and does nothing, because the nations of the Christian fellowship are so jealous of one another, that no one can be allowed to act without incurring the enmity of the rest. And we ask ourselves—can we pray this prayer for ourselves and our families and our own country, without a feeling, deep-seated in our consciences, that somehow the terrible but health-giving judgments of God must fall upon a Christian Europe guilty of this horrible acquiescence? If we do find ourselves punished, and in our distress crying out to a God who seems deaf or powerless, there is one word of an ancient prophet which would certainly apply to us, 'Your sins have withholden good things from you.'

VIII

Forgive us our Debts, as we also have forgiven our Debtors

THERE is no better means of distinguishing true religion from false, than by ascertaining whether its desire is to be redeemed from sin, or to be merely let off from punishment of sin. False religion is everywhere occupied in persuading its God, by means of intercessors or expiatory sacrifices or prayers, to let it off the punishment to which its sins have laid it open. True religion is never occupied with the thought of punishment. Indeed, it recognizes that it is better to be punished when we have done wrong. What it asks is to be rid of the sin itself, its pollution, its guilt, and its power. 'Make me a clean heart, O God, and renew a right spirit within me. Cast me not away from thy presence, and take not thy Holy Spirit from me.' That is always its cry, and the response is always, 'I will sprinkle clean water upon you, and ye shall be clean: a new heart will I give you, and ye shall be my people, and I will be your

God.' This being so, we are pulled up short by this petition in the Lord's Prayer, because at first sight it seems to express just the view of sin which falls short of the truth. It represents the sinner as a debtor who asks to be let off his debts, which, as we know very well, from common experience, is just the request which has least moral reality about it, and involves least moral effort.

We, may think of sin, first of all, as the taint, or flaw, or weakness in our own nature. Considered from this point of view, like the disease or weakness of the body, it cries out for nothing else except actual healing, it admits of no other remedy than that we should again be made whole and strong and full of life. There is no possibility here of our dreaming of being 'let off' without being changed. We can no more be let off our sins than a diseased heart or a defiled blood can be ignored or overlooked. Sins must be healed, and probably by painful remedies.

Secondly, we may think about sin as an offence against our fellow-men. Selfishness, lust, cruelty, injustice, malice, dishonesty, are wrongs against society, and society is quite right in utterly repudiating any idea of forgiving us these things unless we amend and show a disposition to practise the contrary virtues, and make what reparation lies in our power for the wrong that we have done our fellow-men. There ought to be no social forgiveness, except where signs are shown of a new recognition of social duty.

Thirdly, we may regard sin as an offence against God. The character of sin in this relationship is best understood by the wrong which a lawless, rebellious, ungrateful son does to the heart of his father and mother. The hearts of the parents will yearn over their son in any case, but they cannot be satisfied with anything less than some sign of amendment. They will not love him the less for all his outrages. But he cannot come back into the fellowship of home-life (except in a purely external way) unless he shows a change of heart; that is, sorrow for the wrong he has done and the grief he has caused, the sort of sorrow that means amendment for the future—a frank recognition of the laws of home, a loyal obedience to the righteous will which rules there. Looking at sin in these ways, we must pray, Heal our inward diseases, or, Give us a new heart, or, Grant us true conversion of spirit. But sin may also be regarded from a point of view which, in the simplest sense, we may call legal. When a man outrages another's rights, or fails to give him what is his due, society holds him guilty; regards him as under an obligation to restore or to make reparation. And this attitude towards wrong-doing is a reflection of the mind of God. Sin is an outrage upon God's rights—it makes us a debtor; and the debt we can never pay, because we cannot undo the wrong that we have done. Thus, as sin is a debt, the only prayer we can pray is that it shall be remitted: let us off our debt. Are we to say that this is a shallow prayer? Or, occurring as it does in the Lord's Prayer, must we not alter the question, and ask, Why is this not a shallow prayer? I would answer this question thus:—

1. The petition is guarded by the place it holds in the whole. We most naturally put confession of sins and prayer for forgiveness at the beginning of services, but it is very noticeable that in the Lord's Prayer it comes at the end, and to pray the previous clauses of the prayer ensures in the heart of him who offers it everything that is most opposed to a shallow view of forgiveness. No one who has not a changed heart and a new spirit, no one who has not the generosity and nobility of true sonship, can possibly pray that God's name may be hallowed, and His kingdom come, and His will be done.

2. The clause is guarded by what follows it—' As we have forgiven our debtors.' God deals with us as we deal with our fellow-men. There is no possibility, therefore, of this prayer allowing any one to suppose that he can get God to let him off the punishment of his sins and live in the divine favour, while he remains selfish and ungenerous towards his fellow-men. There is no mere insistence upon our rights towards our fellow-men possible, so long as we retain the hope that God is not going to insist on His legal rights towards us. It is only merciful men who can be forgiven.

3. It is evident from all our Lord's teaching in what sense He would have His disciples pray to have their offences forgiven. 'Whom the Lord loveth he chasteneth,' that is, whom the Lord loveth He punisheth. So God is recorded by the Psalmist to have dealt with His saints of old. 'Thou answerest them, O Lord our God; thou art a God that forgavest them, though thou tookest vengeance of their doings.'[1] So it was with 'Moses and Aaron among his priests.' Truly whom the Lord loveth He punisheth. Christ Himself, so far from being exempted from the punishment of human sins, even though the sins were not His own, was conspicuous just for this, that the Lord laid on Him the iniquity of us all, that is, suffered Him to bear the consequences of other men's sins.

There are, we may say, two kinds of punishment for sin. There is the eternal penalty which consists in alienation from God, and that is over when the sinful attitude is over. But there is also the temporal punishment which in the course of nature is so allotted to sin as to follow naturally from it; and when we are forgiven, that becomes the healing chastisement which the penitent heart awaits, with trembling indeed but also with joy. To have our debts remitted then does not mean to be let off all the temporal chastisement due to our sins, but to have in our hearts the

---

[1] Psalm xcix. 8.

consciousness that God has nothing against us—that as He has given us a changed heart, so He has no more in mind the outrages against His majesty and His love of which in the past we have been guilty.

4. To confess the wrongs we have done to the righteousness of God, to own that we cannot undo the past, and then simply to receive of God's undeserved mercy free forgiveness—this is what lays the heart of man under a special sense of gratitude. There is no joyfulness or willingness of service more glad than that of the child who has done wrong and been sorry for it and has been forgiven, and experiences all the rebound of gratitude and love. So the absolved sinner experiences the gratitude of the emancipated heart, emancipated by the simple act of the divine bounty, and the gratitude can show itself in nothing but service.

5. 'Forgive *us* our sins.' There is no forgiveness for ourselves unless we are solicitous that others may be forgiven too. St. John talks about the Christian when 'he sees a brother sin a sin not unto death,' asking God for him and thus obtaining for him the bounty of a fresh gift of spiritual life.[1] Such free interchange of spiritual gifts from brother to brother is not possible where the sin is most grievous—where it is the 'sin unto death'; but where it is, as we say,

[1] St. John v. 16.

a venial sin, there the continual saying of the Lord's Prayer is the winning of a continual and free remission, as for our sins so for the sins of others. Would to God that before we criticize any one of our fellows or our superiors we would say this prayer for him and for ourselves, 'Forgive us our trespasses, as we forgive them that trespass against us.'

Once for all the sacrifice of Christ won for men acceptance with God and forgiveness of their sins. Into that mystery we will not inquire. But we believe that we are admitted within the scope of that forgiveness when we become members of the body of Christ. Out of that holy fellowship we may indeed, by our persistent wilfulness, fall. But so long as we abide in it, we bask altogether in the sunshine of the forgiving love, as a child under the face of his father and his mother, and 'if we confess our sins, he is faithful and just to forgive us our sins, and to cleanse us from all unrighteousness.'

IX

Bring us not into Temptation, but deliver us from the Evil One

I

THE first part of this clause has caused a certain amount of difficulty to thoughtful Christians. For does not St. James bid us count it all joy when we fall into divers temptations, knowing that the trial of our faith worketh patience? How is it then we pray, Lead us not into temptation? To this question one may give a double answer.

1. It has been noticed that our Lord's prayers and words in the hour of His agony before the Passion have a close resemblance to some of the clauses of the Lord's Prayer. 'Not as I will, but as thou wilt.' 'Thy will be done.' 'Watch and pray, that ye enter not into temptation.'[1] And in the prayer following the Last Supper, 'Sanctify (hallow) them in the truth.' 'I made known unto them thy name.' 'I pray that thou

---

[1] St. Matt. xxvi. 39–41.

shouldest keep them from the evil one.'[1]   This being so, it is natural to interpret this particular clause in the Lord's Prayer in the sense of 'Watch and pray, that ye enter` not into temptation.'   Temptation is there treated as the punishment of the carelessness which neglects to watch and pray.   And from this point of view we should naturally interpret 'Lead us not into temptation' thus: Suffer us not to live in spiritual carelessness, so that temptation should come upon us as a snare to our overthrow.   This is a very necessary prayer.   People are very frequently anxious about their spiritual condition when they actually find themselves engulfed in temptation, who have been utterly careless in running into it.   If men in general gave real thought to their truest welfare, it would be impossible for them to pay so little attention to possible spiritual results in making their great choices, such as determine largely the future of their lives.   Thus men rush into a profession generally from no other point of view than that of whether it is likely to pay.   Afterwards they find that their profession subjects their purity or their temperance or their honesty to a strain which is too much for it, and they are full of what is partly complaint and partly horror.   But it might all have been foreseen and guarded against, if, before the choice of their profession, they had prayed the prayer, 'Lead us not into

---

[1] St. John xvii. 11, 15, 26.

temptation.' Exactly the same consideration applies to investing money or to getting married. They are steps which in different degrees involve a man's life in new conditions; and unless he is spiritually a fool, he will 'look' well 'before he leaps' what bearing his new conditions will have upon his life towards God. Exactly the same truth applies to our reading. It is all very well to determine not to be narrow in the literature we read, all very well to know the ways of the world, and to ascertain what people who are not Christians have to say for themselves and against our Creed; but if there is such a thing as spiritual temptation, and a personal responsibility to preserve our innocence and our faith, it is quite certain that there is a way of embarking in the literature of sin and the literature of unbelief which is precisely like walking into an enemy's country in time of war unarmed and unprepared. To pray, 'Lead us not into temptation,' then, involves a corresponding course of action in preparing ourselves against it.

2. But, after all, this explanation of the clause does not exhaust its meaning. It may be God's will that we should not have our daily bread, and yet we have just prayed for it in a previous clause. Thus also it may be God's will that we should be tempted and tried, and yet we may pray that it may not be necessary. We may then, perhaps, paraphrase the prayer—Father, if it be possible, let the cup of temptation pass from me without my drinking it. Some temptation is necessary for

us, but this or that particular temptation may not be necessary, and it may only need a little prayer to enable us to escape it. The wise man knows that he is weak. He can fight, indeed, when fighting is required of him, and find his strength in God; but he will not run into temptation if he can avoid it. He will pray, for others as for himself, 'Lead us not into temptation.'

II

And all this precaution is necessary because, as St. Paul says, 'we wrestle not against flesh and blood, but against principalities, against powers, against the world-rulers of this darkness, against the spiritual forces of wickedness in heavenly places.'[1] In other words, the temptations that come from visible and tangible sources draw their strength from a source which is unseen. Behind visible foes there is an invisible; behind the visible opposition of evil men there is an invisible prince of darkness and an unseen host of fallen spirits intruding themselves into the highest things, into the heavenly places. I am quite sure that our Lord speaks so confidently and so frequently of the existence of evil spirits that a sober Christian cannot doubt their reality,

[1] Eph. vi. 12.

and I feel sure also, that their existence interprets a good deal which would otherwise be unintelligible in our spiritual experience. When thoughts of poisonous evil, distinct and vivid, are shot into our mind, like suggestions from a bad companion; when a tempest of pride and rebellion against God surges over our soul; when voices of discouragement and despair tell us that it is no use trying, and that human nature is hopelessly bad; when a sinful course of action presents itself to us in a wholly false aspect until we have committed ourselves to it, and then strips off its disguises and shows itself in its true colours, in its ugliness, in its treachery, in its infamy—in all such experiences we do well to remember that, besides the weakness or pollution of our own flesh, and besides the solicitations of the world, there is ' the adversary,' ' the devil,' that is, the slanderer of God and of our human nature and the ' father of lies,' actually at work to seduce our wills and sophisticate our intelligences. Moral evil, let us never forget, exists nowhere except in rebellious wills, human or diabolic; and however great the mystery which wraps the ultimate destiny of such rebellious wills, at least we know that their power will have an end, that they will be put manifestly and openly under the feet of Christ, and that the power which by prayer we win here and now, suffices on each occasion to give us strength to triumph againt the devil, as well as the world and the flesh, even as Christ triumphed. For 'this is the victory that overcometh the world, even our faith. Who is he that overcometh the world, but he that believeth that Jesus is the Son of God ?' Yes, God 'will not suffer us on any occasion to be tempted above that we are able, but will with the temptation also make a way to escape, that we may be able to bear it.'[1]

[1] 1 John v. 4 ; 1 Cor. x. 13.

X

[For Thine is the Kingdom, the Power and the Glory, for Ever and Ever]

I

THESE words do not form part of the original text of the Lord's Prayer. They are omitted accordingly in the Revised Version of St. Matt. vi. 13. A doxology, however, closely similar to this was attached to the Lord's Prayer, in the custom of Syrian Christians, before the end of the first century. It is based on David's doxology[1]: 'Thine, O Lord, is the . . . power, and the glory, and . . . the kingdom,' and it·expresses nobly indeed the reason why we pray. God our Father, who is in heaven, has, in spite of all that appears to the contrary, always and everywhere the kingdom, and the power, and the glory. Whatever royalty or power or glory the kingdom of˙evil seems to have to our eyes, as we contemplate the prevalence of lust and worldliness and cruelty and selfishness all around us, is in truth

---

[1] 1 Chron. xxix. 11.

78

but a transitory show, like the imposing glory of Nebuchadnezzar's image of gold in the plain of Dura, of the province of Babylon. There is no real power in it, because its doom is spoken and its overthrow is certain. Therefore there is only one true refuge and strength, and that is God, and only one thing worth having, and that is the life according to God, the life of the Kingdom of God.

II

I have come to the end of this brief explanation of the Lord's Prayer, and I would not add anything, were it not that I have just read in the newspaper a remarkable instance of the difference which I spoke of in an earlier paper between the prayer of instinct and the prayer which is in the name of Christ—the Lord's Prayer. It is well known that Australian primary education has been, speaking generally, purely secular. But recently a much-beloved inspector in South Australia was lying on his death-bed, and an anonymous advertisement in the newspapers, addressed to school-masters, brought it about that one minute before or after regular school hours on a certain day, the children were assembled and requested to repeat off a black-board the words, 'Our Father which art in heaven, grant that our dear master and beloved friend . . . may be restored to health.' Now such a prayer is a remarkable instance of the way in which at any time of imminent calamity the human instinct of prayer will re-assert itself. But it is also a proof that the human instinct does not reach to the point of offering the prayer in Christ's name. The prayer of human instinct is always, 'Give me to-day what I so sorely want,' whereas the prayer which is in the name of Christ starts always from God's point of view, and puts the special need of the individual, of the class, of the country, in its true subordination to the will of God and to the interest of His kingdom. A detached prayer for something we want, apart from any wider or diviner point of view, can never be a prayer in the name of Christ.

May the good God teach us all to pray the Lord's Prayer—and the whole of it—with heart and will and intelligence and voice, in private and in public, in Eucharist and in penitence, for ourselves, for the whole Church, and for all mankind. For he who is ever truly learning to say the Lord's Prayer cannot be far from the kingdom of Heaven, and to say it perfectly is to be in truth a heavenly being already.

WELLS GARDNER, DARTON AND CO., PATERNOSTER BUILDINGS.

Lightning Source UK Ltd.
Milton Keynes UK
UKHW010758221218

334411UK00004B/202/P